THA' MAN WHO MORPHED FROM ADDICTIONS

OVERCOMING LOW INCOME LIVING ADDICTION

ANTONIO A. BURDETTE

Trafford PUBLISHING®   www.trafford.com
North America & international
toll-free: 844-688-6899 (USA & Canada)
fax: 812 355 4082

'VE SEEN SO MANY children who grew up under the government welfare system whose parent clubbed and used drugs frequently and later grew up under a luminous light of depreciation allow me to elaborate neighborhoods that they've spent generations after generation growing up in they embraced the term projects instead of father. Under this light even the youth who appeared to be respectful and mannerable was mixed in the bunch of populated teens running inside and outside of the grounds was no different.

Projects are living quarters that later fell under the stigma of "never having a dull moment" from 5 months 'ol to 12 years 'ol its enclosure influenced you living close nit with another simple arguments that could have been squashed only whined up giving you the number one most rated news channels throughout cities. Funeral homes employees shifts increased and officers of the law became less friendlier when it came to calls within the cast-iron gates.

These low income housing wasn't meant for long term staying it was meant until you were able to get back on your feet. There was a time when no one were hiring and so generations slipped passed without looking back it can now be counted on one hand.

An addict is not just a word to signify a substance abuser when the first piece of crack touch down we became addicts of self-affliction meaning no one family member mattered which means everyone of all ages hung out later and later gathering under street lights like the insects that feeds off the cities energy. I don't have to fabricate or share someone else's life of hustling reason being

I wasn't just a by-stander or on looker. If you could hear your name being called from the doorway you were in close proximity but the reality of it "no one was ready to call it a night the street lights gave structure to why groups cliqued together freestylin' raps and blunt smoking became the norm. Earlier generations respected other people's kids but as years went by they unfortunately got in the way and while blue lights, ambulances and fire trucks lit up the square retaliation from the other generations became an easy initiation and early as it is into this love had nothing to hold it together and the streets became comparison. Comparison in an unprecedented way. I can't say daddies wasn't in these children lives but daddies didn't do much to pull them out of the environment that later cost many their life.

By the time the third generation became teens the projects had gained a title that it would never be able to bounce back from we were labeled as ghetto and ghetto wasn't a word use by the live-in's it came from the suburbs. As I said before there were respectful and well-mannered youth growing up in this but there was no one to give them the structure to ever began straightening out their life.

When it came to the young ladies nice weather brought about the short shorts and tops which revealed little to the imagination. 'Til this day I can't wrap my mind around why this type of living was a magnet to neighborhoods nearby. Older men would come out and drink from the bottle, grill out, and play cards for hours. While in the meantime abstinence wasn't being taught and by the end of summer plenty whined up pregnant and keep in mind crack is now used and bout to bring about a change.

A party atmosphere is just that….a party. It didn't matter if the project was up north, down south, large or small it for sure wasn't asleep and neither were the toddlers who occupied the sidewalks and the middle age bicycling in the streets.

Because jobs were few people vehicles became less manageable to maintenance and so they became resting spots for the much older kids to lean against and sit on. When I say this I say with all due respect the project should never be aligned with a zoo because zoos categorize they residence according to same species projects are living quarters with different mindsets and upbringing. After making a couple sells of crack ones pocket is starting to bulge and the number of samplers are on a mission walking back and forth apparently the high is a short one most of 'em walking up with the money in they hand a red flag I knew to stay away from just because of the traffic it was generating but it didn't stop me from selling the less harmless of the drugs.

When it comes to living within these stomping grounds everyone is so caught up interacting with one another that no one paying attention and not paying attention can be detrimental and I can't use detrimental without having a lump in my throat.

Kids were struck by cars riding bikes, kids were struck with bullets just being in the crossfire, arguments turned into street fights and toddlers can be found 3 apartment doors down from where they live and loud music from cars and outside are house speakers placed on the lawn giving life to the rugged atmosphere. One couldn't keep it to himself how much he been making pumping the crack so in order to avoid the jealousy they become partners and now guns are needed for anybody else who might wanna eyeball what the fast money brought. Not all parents were on section 8 some worked extremely long hours just to try and make a decent paycheck but the downside to that was they were never home so the boys flirted more and the girls gave-in giving a new name to a younger woman in her 30's they either go by Gam'ma or Na'na either way it wasn't planned. Young and pregnant and being told that she's a high risk pregnancy she couldn't contribute much and so for a while she holds down a generational spot some did good having only one baby daddy and some had more than one but the late night phone conversations with the back and forth who she really wanna be with brought about a whole lot of turmoil when they eventually crossed paths these were supposed to be the men to help plan and motivate her future but it mostly brought about arguments and fighting and more guns. A good meal could be smelled all throughout the hallways but a night out clubbing something always manage to get cooked and left on the stove and a small grease fire brings cops and fire trucks back out to light up the scene for the already late nighters who just sitting out enjoying the night air.

Don't be fool by everything you read or see on T.V. there are good people that grow up in these living quarters they are the ones who very seldom get into trouble and the cops never seem to come out on a call involving them. Let me make this clear they are the eyes and ears of the set but they are not snitches and we never question them because they do try hard to hold on to that humbleness that so many others refuse to grasp.

One thing is for certain living within the gates you will find yourself socializing in groups and the thing about a group it always give off the impression that you're doing something you shouldn't be doing or y'all up to no good and a lot of the time it's just conversation and making your swag official a lot of the time it's just good conversation and I interpreted it as what I consider "WILD'lin" would fathers have made a difference and the answer to that would have been yes. You wouldn't have witness 5-9 year 'ol standing in the middle lane of the road attempting to get to the Cornerstore. People would pretty much laugh and grin about anything but is it possible to have happiness within tha' set? For me it was no but I did venture off enough to not block my blessings completely I met girls who lived in nice homes with their parents, I worked the type of jobs where I can mingle with the girls occasionally and still make a paycheck and I went without a lot of things even though the crack selling era was booming growin' up in this uncertain habitat a reputation was required and I used "was" instead of "is" because everyone felt it was necessary to have one except the respectful and mannerable ones. I was known being low-key worked in my favor and I'll explain why before cellphones videos swept the nation the news media was on the scene and they came to report and document and a lot of the project residents felt it was a good time to be on T.V. even though they were out there because of someone spassing on another but so much was once again captured the children playing unattended, the liquor bottle on the card table, the samplers walking in one direction and the medics tending to the victim you could hear loud music blaring out of cars circling through and those that made up your circle wanted they shot to be on the news for a lack of better words "Looking Fo' Street Cred."

On a nice sunny day it's a must that you fire the grill up and invite a few of your friends surprisingly when they do pull up it's a car full of their friends whom you may have met at least once or twice and they jumpin' out with bottles and cases of beer and packs of cigars waiting to get bust down and smoked and that's why projects stay pack because everyone think in the same way just to avoid having a dull moment, me writing this is far from living-in-the moment depending on who you are it's a blessing and a curse. The blessing is surviving throughout the year and the curse is watching the kids become young addicts by what they see and the life that they are exposed too.

What I'm about to say could and should be examine there are some literature that will say that Satan controls the airwaves and if you listed to different broadcasts coming from the many apartments you might find some truth in that maybe some shows are edited in a slow-dragging tempo or maybe the spirit of the slain cry out and go where its excepted it's just a theory but you have to pay attention to the other addiction that was hard to escape living there vigils. Vigils came about often and it never allowed anyone to heal completely it was like a reset button and there was always someone there to push it.

One of the things that appaused me was when a couple would argue and fight. It would cause everyone to come out of their living quarters and watch but what was more shocking they proceeded as if no one was outside watching the set and location I'm preferrin' to there wasn't much to do and when school would let out for the summer the grounds stayed packed and by the time summer set-in good people in this set had already had a look about them that the public would take and run with.

Why must it seem like everything they did seem as if it was stereotyping them because a motorize dirt bike is meant for the track it was seen ripping and running all day throughout the day loud music had just captivated the scene you would find people building speaker boxes that would hold 12" woofers with powerful amps that would cause them to jump out of the box but what I quickly notice that when they pulled up beside someone at a red light. They would get that stare of disbelief and no one ever thought to just turn it down just alil while at the light and again it caught the city attention and a citation was issued if you were stopped by the law a healthy one of $50-$100 and 'til this day it remain popular even I like my music loud but not $50-$100 loud to each his own.

Each set was given a grounds keeper to keep the trash from cluttering up the neighborhood and it most certainly was a recommended line of work not everything made it in the dumpster and many new faces were seen replacing the previous one and the question is this can you hold a child responsible because his or her upbringing didn't have that extra voice of strictness to began planting that seed? Single mothers haven't just started getting tired but it seem like they had no cut off almost as if tunnel vision had set in all they know is that they had to keep going and working to provide and between the two man and female no one can match her determination to just stay afloat in a honest way. Every family has that one member who has done well for themselves not saying it was the case with me but I would've strongly preferred to relocate but everything that I observed it taught me to always want better for myself and what type of woman would be best to suit me. It took live-in experiences with a woman that had good clean qualities but her attitude was my reason to exit the commitment and vice versa I too was a sponge. Neighborhoods around the city became so active that if you were

walking to the cornerstore or just in a group

with 2 or more people cops would just roll-up

on you asking for your I.D. and frisk you if

they felt it was necessary and that irritated

my age group and most of them did not see

that as a small wake-up calling they did the

opposite they provoked them and it was up to

you to grasp the concept what came from that

a lot more young adults were arrested with

simple charges instead of just being released

to go bout they business.

One year the gun violence had gotten so

bad that they issued a city curfew and when

it came to the curfew I took my chances but I

did things different and the reason I complied and did things different because it was a harmless mandate nothing good comes from rippin' and runin' every time someone calls and need you it's a hard lesson and many fail to once again grasp that concept.

Cop cars were heavy in the streets and if you were pulled over you were asked where you were going or where you coming from? And your answer determine if you drove off or rode with them. Holidays that required fireworks most times I was working or I simply just stayed home either way you heard both.

What was special but not noticed I was working alongside these women who was carrying everyone else baggage and living within these gates.

I recall a time that a child found where someone hid their pistol the cops were called and the pistol was removed and it's that type of negligence that would've led to a fatality. A lot of what I'm saying in this attention-seeking guide was a while ago but by you just seeing snippets of it on the news I felt that if I went back and relived the younger adults can avoid making some mistake by not gravitating toward the group sessions. If you don't remember anything else remember this it doesn't matter how well you may know an individual you have to plan your own future set your own goals and motivate yourself because the other person they know how far they gonna go and the assumption is for you to stop whenever they do and what sometimes seems like enough most times isn't.

You have to come to the conclusion that if you simply take the less paying job offered it'll plant the seed when it comes to collecting at the end of the year. You shouldn't just want to see others doing good for themselves driving the nicer cars, wearing the latest name brand you have to have the mindset to live better and not let the job always dictate why you're not home to supervise your child I witnessed it I lived it and I know how it brought about strong feelings when it came to me why I couldn't attend certain functions or just spend quality time with my kids. Addiction is a self-afflicted habit and its rooted by the unwelcome scenarios that allows you to think that taking short cuts are o.k.

Each and every novel that I write its to give her a financial jumpstart to recover from the hardship of holding the title of provider example my wife is one of the hardest working woman I know she holds a senior cook position in a retirement home and she's always there her shift ended and her car wouldn't start after the fact we paid on some other bills but I heard the frustration in her voice and I see the look of concern on her face having to go without when it comes to the scripture as for me and my house we were able to fix the problem with the help of a honest mobil mechanic who over all seen the big picture of who we are... as individuals and I was able to put something in his pockets.

The more I was participating in the things going on around me and not focusing on having a good work ethic I was becoming a less appreciative individual and that mentality would've made me just another crab in the bucket so instead of preventing another one from escaping I can now be an asset in someone's life only you know what its like to have to live-in that moment and have to deal with the adversities which lie ahead without warning it only take a few with the improper upbringing to influence a group to ignore their basic principals even though I was silently screaming on the inside I wanted someone to rescue me but what's more rewarding than seeing your accomplishments because you had to get tired of a situation or predicament to simply desire better.

One thing I realized your life doesn't have to be no more complicated than you make it I grew up in a countryish environment with (5) relatives it was just us as people marry into families they bring along all they flaws as well I speak and write from experience but in order to begin giving myself a little bit of credit I set the foundation the only way you will get to know me is by my works and each unpredictable day that the Lord allow me to awake and arise in a upright position is all the motivation I need and it's not just the children growing up in the rugged habitat who need to be reminded that they have not been counted out if you go throughout your whole day without picking up a book or just learning a fact by googling how will you be benefitting the younger generation when that was our calling from the beginning what type of person are you? Will you sit at the table get a full stomach and afterward head to the couch and catch the last quarters of the game or will you walk a mile and a half return spruce up the yard before you cross the bridge of getting comfortable? Being comfortable is not everybody's main objective. Some of us we know that we will have to eventually become a fill-in a temp employee if you will but its what the heart says and not the expectation of receiving a reward.

There's one generation that took it upon themselves to teach values and everything after that was I said, go get that, what's your problem, don't make me and none of these has the power to instill its just the use of authority being said indirectly and they are repeated so often 'til its what they expect teachers, coaches and a lot of authority figures try hard to reset how some things should be addressed and translated a child growing up in a low income housing setting they absolutely have a beautiful quality but the teacher vs. the parent leaves the child to interact within their outside world among their peers even as a child you know the difference between being poor and middle class I only know of one organization who tried to instill and break the stronghold of settling comfortably before an inappropriate time and that was JTPA and I can speak on that because I attended and I worked and by the end of the summer I was successful molded enough to be considered a responsible young adult. So all hope isn't loss it has to be others to continue the hereditary trade 13 years old is a reasonable age to began having a sufficient amount in a bank account being human it's a must you have funds its easy for our teens to get a hold of their first vehicle but if no one teaches them that insurance has to remain on that vehicle and that their license has to be valid and a sudden traffic stop doesn't have to be the next news headline because if all the correct information is up to date a sudden stop and procedure shouldn't spook the driver and their passenger we got to get back to doing somethings in a simple manner. I guess what I'm trying to say is that children growing up in the low income housing in a single parent home are not your daily quotas that has to be met teach young adults that you can't just jump in a car every time one crank-up by the number of heads it will certainly increase the chances to use force against someone for an authority figure to use force against another is a tunnel vision mentality and from standing behind the badge a simple request to be asked to comply probably won't get asked any nicer sit 'em down and have the talk stop holding on to that I'm loyal to my boys mentality if the cops pull up on you comply immediately put your hands up because if you have nothing on you, you should have no problem answering their questions and complying.

If a person in your group has a bag of weed on him if it wasn't smoked before the cops rolled up you are not obligated to take his charge that's considered his personal and it doesn't tie you to a misjudgment or assumption that it was about to get used parents as long as it's you talking to your child they yes Ma'am I understand but when the pressure is really applied all that goes out the window small stores sell toy badges with the cuffs you have to get another adult to pretend to be so that you'll see just how he'll act when you are not around and a toy badge isn't noticeable in the sight of a child to know the difference.

I've watch movies where an innocent man is being questioned about either drugs or murder but he dances around the fact that it's not his or he didn't do it and whined up falsely accused you have (2) ways to claim your innocent through questioning or written statements and if you refuse to tell the truth in a written statement changing your mind when you're locked up is a little too late. You chose to become a being told what to do man. The scenarios mention in this guide are not habits. They are addictions daily addictions and they have to be addressed differently because they are not the same problems biblical generations made 100's of centuries ago and in the same manner God will step-in with results in the same way we have to first address them and wait for his approval.

Young adults are driven by not having a sit still moment and fun but we know too much fun only ends up in fatalities at some point we have to intercept from allowing low budget scripted actors who only portraying to be thugs manipulating the only 3D image of creation that we know we made we are not living in the times where vigils are caused by natural deaths and its vigils residents within these cast-iron gates has dealt with over and over again which gives them the notation that they will be next and it won't be of a natural cause.

Society alone can be a vindictive demon. If by word of mouth that you hear of this manuscript allow your child to read it to you to balance the understanding and listen to what catches their attention. Again I'm not driven by the force of a dollar it's more rewarding that I can use my hard earn money to document facts from the street side of things which speaks volumes on my behalf.

All project management need to hold themselves accountable and take the initiative to control how populated an enclosure could get tenants are still paying rent to be able to sit on their stoops without all the extra commotion.

Projects and when you think of them you immediately think of a killing field and that's far from the truth when toddlers and middle age children should be the focus. I made advances in my life because I was tired of being the problem and being a problem amongst so many only puts you in the sight of someone dying to solve 'em. It don't matter if you rap or write your testimony it only means that you're ready for the next chapter in your life with the ultimate concern to embrace the ones coming after you. When we meaning adults are faced with a life threatening encounter lying in the hospital bed we hoping and wishing for an instant prayer to just have one more chance "I promise I'll do a lot of things different." But you never address the fact that you should have said or done what was needed to have your work to speak for you. This luminous light of deappreciation which hover the projects sometimes hidden by dark clouds will still be there even when they pass. Will we allow the right to own guns to speak so loud and boldly that it gives proof to why the cemeteries are the quietest places on earth but are the most well-kept in appearances. Our children are being laid to rest with the first fruits who knew that family values were the life-saving elements to become recognizable as civilized.

To the readers of this you shouldn't feel ashamed to have endued the hardship which leaves you feeling indecisive about who you are anything documented or script into an award winning real life thriller is fruit growing on a curse tree. A good parent can only give the approval to avoid why the fruit is forbidden and if you except what it has to offer the end of the movie will only give you another comfortable ending into the next scripted beginning of why low income lives are taken for granted. I can't take from the selective few who are rooting for you to decline on mischievous invitations but you have to speak louder than the gunshots and we have to intervene and separate what's for adults and what's for children. Don't become too strict that you become naïve children are entitled to make mistakes when facing addiction head on. It's gonna require a lot of professional assistance and willingness by the victims who manage to live passed it remember your testimony will engage you into a new life under God's approval.

You can't have that ghetto mentality to hustle drugs or anything else that the low income revealed. I spend a lot of quiet time preparing what is to be documented for the sake or developing minds. Don't ask for prayers to be answered and because he chose to use me to relay information that has slipped through grown up hands for years. 2021 is quite a distance from the early 60's lace up your boots because we are about to handle any future setbacks head-on. Titles that has plagued low-income living the vindictive acts of domestic violence, murderers, thieves, drug dealin', pedophiles, child abusers, can't just be swept under the rug these titles has to be explained and broken down.

For the younger minds and in the eyes of society and those who hold authority stay applying the pressure of your city citizens to do what's necessary and a simple agreement makes all the difference. At one time my age group thought that they wouldn't make it to see 25 and as people whined up missing and dead they calmed down and took hold of what the bible would consider "humble". But in order for that to happen your whereabouts became a precaution. What is it gonna take for your generation? A $10 book can be what makes all the difference in your child's life cause the negative energy is a force and it has persuaded time after time between a book and loaded gun that a loaded gun can be handled.

Printed in the United States
by Baker & Taylor Publisher Services